W9-BYA-981

ZOO CLUES

My Nose Is Long and Fuzzy

by Joyce Markovics

Consultants:
Christopher Kuhar, PhD
Executive Director
Cleveland Metroparks Zoo
Cleveland, Ohio

Kimberly Brenneman, PhD
National Institute for Early Education Research
Rutgers University
New Brunswick, New Jersey

BEARPORT PUBLISHING

New York, New York

Credits

Cover, © ZSSD/Minden Pictures/Corbis; 4–5, © Ardea/Watson, M./Animals Animals;
6–7, © Therin–Weise/Arco Images GmbH; 8–9, © National Geographic Image
Collection/Alamy; 10–11, © Roberto Tetsuo Okamura/Shutterstock; 12–13, © ZSSD/
Minden Pictures/Corbis; 14–15, © Christian Musat/Shutterstock; 16–17, © Luciano
Candisani/Getty Images; 18–19, © Ardea/Watson, M./Animals Animals/Earth
Scenes; 20–21, © Ardea/Watson, M./Animals Animals/Earth Scenes; 22, © Christian
Musat/Shutterstock; 23, © iStockphoto/Thinkstock; 24, © iStockphoto/Thinkstock.

Publisher: Kenn Goin
Senior Editor: Joyce Tavolacci
Creative Director: Spencer Brinker
Design: Debrah Kaiser
Photo Researcher: Michael Win

Library of Congress Cataloging-in-Publication Data

Markovics, Joyce L.
  My nose is long and fuzzy / by Joyce Markovics ; consultant: Christopher Kuhar, PhD,
Executive Director, Cleveland Metroparks Zoo, Cleveland, Ohio.
      pages cm. — (Zoo clues)
  Includes bibliographical references and index.
  ISBN-13: 978-1-62724-111-3 (library binding)
  ISBN-10: 1-62724-111-6 (library binding)
  1. Myrmecophaga—Juvenile literature. I. Title.
  QL737.E24M37 2014
  599.3'14—dc23
                              2013035384

For more information, write to Bearport Publishing Company, Inc., 45 West 21st Street, Suite 3B,
New York, New York 10010. Printed in the United States of America.

10 9 8 7 6 5 4 3 2 1

What Am I?

Look at my tail.

Contents

It is large
and bushy.

5

My claws are
sharp and curved.

I have stiff hairs
on my back.

My ears are
small and round.

My nose is long
and fuzzy.

I have a black-and-white stripe on my body.

15

I have a long,
pink tongue.

What am I?

Let's find out!

I am a giant anteater!

Animal Facts

Giant anteaters are mammals. Like almost all mammals, giant anteaters give birth to live young. The babies drink milk from their mothers. Mammals also have hair or fur on their skin.

More Giant Anteater Facts

Food:	Ants and termites
Size:	5 to 7 feet (1.5 to 2 m) long from nose to tail
Weight:	60 to 140 pounds (27 to 64 kg)
Life Span:	14 years
Cool Fact:	A giant anteater's tongue can be more than 19 inches (48 cm) long!

Adult Giant Anteater Size

Where Do I Live?

Giant anteaters live in forests and grasslands in Central and South America.

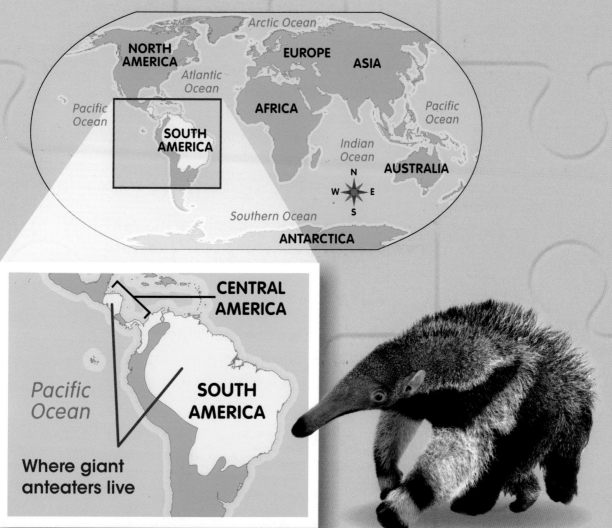

Arctic Ocean

NORTH AMERICA

EUROPE

ASIA

Atlantic Ocean

Pacific Ocean

AFRICA

Pacific Ocean

SOUTH AMERICA

Indian Ocean

AUSTRALIA

N W E S

Southern Ocean

ANTARCTICA

CENTRAL AMERICA

Pacific Ocean

SOUTH AMERICA

Where giant anteaters live

Index

Read More

Antill, Sara. *Giant Anteaters (Unusual Animals).* New York: Windmill Books (2011).

Gillenwater, Chadwick. *Giant Anteaters (Pebble Plus: South American Animals).* North Mankato, MN: Capstone (2012).

Learn More Online

To learn more about giant anteaters, visit
www.bearportpublishing.com/ZooClues

About the Author

Joyce Markovics lives along the Hudson River in Tarrytown, New York. She enjoys spending time with furry, finned, and feathered creatures.